WHY AMERICA SHOULD
JOIN THE ALLIES

WHY AMERICA SHOULD JOIN THE ALLIES

BY

THEODORE ROOSEVELT.

❧Juniper Grove❧

This book has been reprinted from the
1915 C. Arthur Pearson Ltd. edition.

Juniper Grove
ISBN 978-1-60355-071-0
©2007 Juniper Grove

PUBLISHERS' NOTE.

Every hour the question of America's neutrality becomes more acute. We are so used to regarding Americans as our own flesh and blood that we lose sight of the fact that there are in the United States twenty million people of German birth—many of them occupying very influential positions—who are striving hard to foster in Americans a strong feeling on behalf of Germany. The danger of this influence is fully realised by Mr. Theodore Roosevelt, the ex-President of the United States, and he is using his best endeavours to counteract it by advocating that America should join the Allies in the present war. He has written a powerful article embodying his arguments, which we have secured for publication in this country. In order to facilitate a proper understanding of his attitude we present, first of all, a statement concerning the feeling in America at the moment, and append those extracts from the Act of the Second Peace Conference at the Hague which have bearing on Mr. Roosevelt's words.

A
WORD OF EXPLANATION.

To the ordinary Englishman with a turn for politics the view-point of the United States is one of profound importance in the present War crisis. There is no general expectation in this country to-day that America will take any active part in the hostilities either on the side of Germany and Austria or the Allies, but there is everywhere a growing desire that the real truth about the conflict should emerge from the present welter of misunderstanding and misstatement, and that the most powerful neutral country in the world should appreciate not only the outrages that have been committed in the facile and easily misunderstood name of "Kultur," but its own duties in the light of its solemn obligations, and as seen through the eyes of the civilised world.

It is a matter of common knowledge now that when the War actually broke out in August the attitude of the United States was the subject of considerable speculation and doubt. Unlike the contradictory history of the relations between England and America, the records of the dealings between Washington and Berlin exhibited a series of friendly negotiations and concessions that no negotiations over commercial treaties, no influx of millions upon millions of sturdy German emigrants, no heart-burning over sundry high-handed interpretations of the Monroe Doctrine in South America had ever been able to dim. For years, in view of this War, the Kaiser had nursed American public opinion in his favour with all the zeal and the cunning and the assiduity of an American press-agent. Nothing had been too high for the All-highest War Lord—even the gift of sundry Bibles to sundry churches. Nothing had been too low for him —even the visit to New York of his own great Sea Lord, Prince Henry of Prussia, who promptly went to law with his American dentist. Behind every move in his game stood sinister figures of the secret agents and spies of the Wilhelmstrasse—men who took care to acquire powerful influence in such German-American cities as Milwaukee, Cincinnati, and St. Louis, and to sway that influence on political and social lines in the

8

direction of Germany to the limit of their purses and their power.

Finally the hour struck. The figures of great Jewish German financiers emerged from their customary seclusion in New York, Chicago, and other big American cities, and these money-making patriots boldly lent to Germany out of the coffers of the United States the millions she required to launch her world campaign with a decent promise of success. In those times Germany and her friends in distant places had more to hope from the turn of the cards than they have at present. Most of all, perhaps, they had reason to build good hopes on the fact that the Democrats were in power in United States politics—for did not the Democrats stand for Tammany Hall for many years longer than most of them to-day would care to recall, and neither in proverb nor in song nor in actual practice had the Democrat and Bribery and Corruption ever been seriously divorced.

Quick-witted and keen to realise the importance of American right-thinking at that juncture, Mr. Winston Churchill permitted himself to be interviewed by the representative of an American news syndicate early in August. As is his habit, the First Lord of the Admiralty did not on that occasion mince his words. "Depend upon it," he said in effect to the great American nation, "you are not so little interested in the issue of this conflict as the majority of your public men pretend to affect. To-day we are in the firing-line alongside of the French, the Belgians, and the Russians. Remember this, if we fail—it is your turn next."

It would be refreshing and consoling to be able to add that the United States took this semi-paternal advice from one of the youngest and most prominent of her gifted stepsons with becoming anxiety and reverence—but, unfortunately, nothing of the sort happened. America duly ranged herself alongside of the other neutral nations, and the American newspapers talked Neutrality with such awe and carefulness and power of iteration that impartial onlookers began to believe there must be some potent magic hidden in the mere expression of the word. It is easy, however, to declare neutrality at the entrance to a quarrel. The real pinch comes when things begin to happen. Hence, when, in defiance of the Hague Convention to which the United States were parties no less than Germany, poor Belgium was invaded and sacked, her cities were laid desolate, her girls and women subjected to unspeakable outrage, and her people terrorised, robbed, blackmailed, and starved, America began, in her own language, to sit up and to take notice.

Belgium and England and France will always remember with gratitude the great wave of sympathy that apparently swept over the United States following these discoveries. It took expression in many strange and weird and unexpected forms, but, undoubtedly, it was real and true; and conscious that it was genuine and not pinchbeck, the Allies turned to their first and most important task—the reduction of the enemy, convinced that now the heart of the United States beat true and sound. It is, however, almost ancient history now that Belgium and her friends at this juncture acted without any of the long long thoughts that diplomacy in America always warrants. They certainly did not realise that the psychology of the American people was one that was largely under the influence of the newest impressions; and soon Berlin despatched Press embassies that painted the chief American cities snowy white with accounts of German gentleness, sweetness, light, and Kultur.

Behind the scenes Americans of German origin worked with frantic energy and zeal over the same mission. Papers and politicians were bombarded with facts "made in Germany," and even crowds in the streets in homely homespuns, engrossed in the bulletin boards, were harangued by these eager missionaries of German reasonableness and peacefulness. The Allies issued various Blue Books that set out in clear and unmistakable terms the real facts about the origin of the quarrel—but a German lie is of a peculiarly facile and agile species, and unfortunately, as events proved, these German lies about the criminality of Belgium and the rest of the Allies got several weeks' start of the truth. The Americans collected—and to their everlasting credit are still collecting—millions of dollars for the relief of the starving Belgians. But the German-American population of the

United States rapidly grew aggressively active, so that bit by bit sides began to be taken on the other side of the Atlantic; the accuracy of the news supplied from centres outside Berlin was slowly and insidiously disputed; and to-day in the United States there are two compact and powerful but utterly distinct bodies of opinion—those who hold Germany is a victim (a body composed chiefly of aliens hostile to Great Britain) and those who believe Germany is the aggressor, a hopeless barbarian, and that she deserves to be irretrievably crushed.

A powerful section in this last-named body also raises a question of far-reaching importance to England and her Allies. It is this: Are the United States justified in doing nothing when the Hague Convention, to which they gave their solemn signature and assent, is outraged by Germany in almost every fibre—when a neutral country which all the parties have undertaken to protect is invaded by one of their number, defenceless cities are bombarded without notice, and heavy cash demands are made upon inhabitants whom the invaders have driven to starvation?

13

It does not, however, follow that the United States will continue as a matter of course to permit Germany to flout the Convention to which the American people, through their chosen representatives, have pledged their solemn honour. Various public men in America have taken up this aspect of the question with characteristic warm-heartedness and thoroughness, not the least prominent of whom is Mr. Theodore Roosevelt, who discusses the problem with great clearness, frankness, and fairness in the following pages.

Mr. William Jennings Bryan (to whom Mr. Roosevelt refers) is the present American Secretary of State. He was Democratic candidate for the Presidency of the United States in 1896, 1900, and 1908, while Mr. William Taft was, it will be remembered, Mr. Roosevelt's direct successor as Republican President, but was previously American Secretary of War.

It would be worse than a mistake—it would be also a blunder of the first magnitude —to under-estimate the importance of Mr. Roosevelt in the public eye and thought of America. In his recently-published work on

14

"American Public Opinion," Mr. James Davenport Whelpley says frankly that the younger Wing of the Republican party, " the Progressives, led by Theodore Roosevelt, is resting hopefully and confidently in the conviction that its intrepid political warrior will in good time lead it to victory. In brief, there are but two dominant Forces in American politics to-day: one is Woodrow Wilson, President, and the other is Theodore Roosevelt, ex-President, who plans to return to the White House later on ! "

President Wilson is also the subject of some criticism. Some newspapers allege he is unconsciously influenced by the German-Jewish-American financiers who provided Germany with the sinews of war, and that as an ex-college professor he has too much of that professorial mind that drove Germany *viá* the school and university into its present saturnalia of superman arrogance, barbarism, and destruction. Yet nothing has yet happened between this country and the United States. to justify such a charge.

It would be a pity, however, to expect too soon anything in the shape of a new heaven or a new earth to spring up as the result of Mr. Roosevelt's ideas. Mr. Whelpley, for instance, quotes the well-known saying of a prominent Englishman who, when he was congratulated upon the good relations which then existed between the English and American peoples, shrugged his shoulders and said, " Yes, they are very good now, but how long will they remain so ? We are always the same, but American public sentiment changes so easily and so often ! " And he goes on to remind us : " There is one important fact which has been learned by American visitors to England and conveyed to those who have stayed at home, which has not yet been fully grasped either by British visitors to America or English people who have never visited America, and that is that the two peoples are separate and distinct nationalities, with different mental habits and different points of view. The English are as they were. From the American melting-pot has come metal of a different alloy which has run into a mould not of English manufacture.

" No harm has come out of this difference in nationality, and, when it is realised," he adds, "good will result, for Americans and English alike will not assume that they are the same people, and act accordingly—generally to their mutual confusion."

Mr. Roosevelt, however, in the following pages speaks some strong and convincing words on the part that America ought to take in the present conflict in Europe, and it may easily happen that a violent agitation may follow his utterances. The American people are a curious mixture of business qualities and rabid sentimentality, and, for some reasons, it is a pity nobody can ever be quite sure whether commercial considerations, or the flat-footed brand of sentimentalism will rule their finer feelings on the morrow. The pro-Germans are staking all on the reputed American tenderness for the dollar. It is within the bounds of possibility they may find that they had relied too much on native selfishness ; it would not be the first time within the past six months that they have had to learn a similar lesson. As Mr. Whelpley points out: "The popularity of Mr. Roosevelt and his hold upon the American people have been gained through his courageous attacks upon established

17   B

injustice," and it may quite easily happen that this particular courageous attack in his article may supply the momentum to a revolution which may lead some thoughtful Germans to realise how that crude monster Prussian military autocracy looks when it is naked and unashamed, and even indicate the foundations upon which the warring Powers of Europe might quite reasonably evolve Peace.

At all events, Mr. Roosevelt's words on the subject will repay the most careful consideration, not only in the United States, but also in the Old World. Time alone will show whether they have been strong enough to light the torch that will guide the consciences of American politicians into the obvious paths of International Rectitude and Justice.

STANHOPE W. SPRIGG.
(*Formerly New York Correspondent of the London* STANDARD).

WHY AMERICA SHOULD JOIN THE ALLIES

BY

THEODORE ROOSEVELT.

" War is Hell."

—*General Sherman.*

WHY AMERICA SHOULD JOIN THE ALLIES.

SHERMAN's celebrated declaration about war has certainly been borne out by what has happened in Europe, and above all in Belgium, during the last four months. That war is hell I will concede as heartily as any ultra-pacificist. But the only alternative to war, that is to hell, is the adoption of some plan substantially like that which I have advocated and which has itself been called Utopian. It is possible that it is Utopian for the time being; that is, that nations are not ready as yet to accept it. But it is also possible that after this war has come to an end the European contestants will be sufficiently sobered to be willing to consider some such proposal.

The proposal is not in the least Utopian if by Utopian we understand something that is theoretically desirable but impossible. What I propose is a working and realisable Utopia. My proposal is that the efficient civilised nations—those that are efficient in war as well as in peace—shall join in a world league for the peace of righteousness. This means that they shall by solemn covenant agree as to their respective rights which shall not be questioned; that they shall agree that all other questions arising between them shall be submitted to a court of arbitration; and that they shall also agree—and here comes the vital and essential point of the whole system—to act with the combined military strength of all of them against any recalcitrant nation, against any nation which transgresses at the expense of any other nation the rights which it is agreed shall not be questioned, or which on matters that are arbitrable refuses to submit to the decree of the arbitral court.

PUT FORCE BACK OF RIGHTEOUSNESS.

In its essence this plan means that there

shall be a great international treaty for the peace of righteousness; that this treaty shall explicitly secure to each nation and except from the operations of any international tribunal such matters as its territorial integrity, honour, and vital interest, and shall guarantee it in the possession of these rights; that this treaty shall therefore by its own terms explicitly provide against making foolish promises which cannot and ought not to be kept; that this treaty shall be observed with absolute good faith—for it is worse than useless to enter into treaties until their observance in good faith is efficiently secured.

Finally, and most important, this treaty shall put force back of righteousness, shall provide a method of securing by the exercise of force the observance of solemn international obligations. This is to be accomplished by all the powers covenanting to put their whole strength back of the fulfilment of the treaty obligations, including the decrees of the court established under and in accordance with the treaty.

23

ASSAULT AND ARBITRATION.

This proposal, therefore, meets the well-found objections against the foolish and mischievous all-inclusive arbitration treaties recently negotiated by Mr. Bryan under the direction of President Wilson. These treaties, like the all-inclusive arbitration treaties which President Taft started to negotiate, explicitly include as arbitrable or as proper subjects for action by joint commissions questions of honour and of vital national interest. No such provision should be made. No such provision is made as among private individuals in any civilised community.

If in private life one individual takes action which immediately jeopardises the life or limb or even the bodily well-being and the comfort of another, the wronged party does not have to go into any arbitration with the wrongdoer. On the contrary, the policeman or constable or sheriff immediately and summarily arrests the wrongdoer. The subsequent trial is not in the nature of arbitration at all. It is in the nature of a criminal proceeding. The wronged man is merely a witness and not necessarily an essential witness.

For example, if, in the streets of New York, one man assaults another or steals his watch, and a policeman is not near by, the wronged man is not only justified in knocking down the assailant or thief, but fails in his duty if he does not so act. If a policeman is near by, the policeman promptly arrests the wrongdoer. The magistrate does not arbitrate the question of property rights in the watch nor anything about the assault. He satisfies himself as to the facts and delivers judgment against the offender.

LET US HAVE PLAIN SPEAKING.

A covenant between the United States and any other power to arbitrate all questions, including those involving national honour and interest, neither could nor ought to be kept. Such a covenant will be harmless only if no such questions ever arise. All the worth of promises made in the abstract lies in the way in which they are fulfilled in the concrete.

Mr. Bryan's arbitration treaties are to be tested in this manner. His theory is, of course, that these treaties are to be made with all nations, and this is correct, because it would be a far graver thing to refuse to make them with some nations than to refuse to enter into them with any nation at all. The proposal is, in effect, and disregarding verbiage, that all questions shall be arbitrated or settled by the action of a joint commission—questions really vital to us would, as a matter of fact, be settled adversely to us pending such action.

There are many such questions which in the concrete we would certainly not arbitrate. I mention one, only as an example.

Does Mr. Bryan, or does he not, mean to arbitrate, if Japan should so desire, requesting whether Japanese labourers are to be allowed to come in unlimited numbers to these shores? If he does mean this, let him explicitly state that fact—merely as an illustration—to the

Senate committee, so that the Senate committee shall understand what it is doing when it ratifies these treaties.

If he does not mean this, then let him promptly withdraw all the treaties so as not to expose us to the charge of hypocrisy, of making believe to do what we have no intention of doing, and of making promises which we have no intention of keeping.

I have mentioned one issue only; but there are scores of other issues which I could mention in which this Government would under no circumstances agree to arbitrate.

WORTHLESS PEACE CONGRESSES.

In the same way, we must explicitly recognise that all the peace congresses and the like that have been held of recent years have done no good whatever to the cause of world peace. All their addresses and resolutions about arbitration and disarmament and such matters have been on the whole slightly worse than useless. Disregarding the Hague conven-

27

tions, it is the literal fact that none of the peace congresses that have been held for the last fifteen or twenty years—to speak only of those of which I myself know the workings— have accomplished the smallest particle of good.

In so far as they have influenced free, liberty-loving and self-respecting nations not to take measures for their own defence they have been positively mischievous. In no respect have they achieved anything worth admiring; and the present world war proves this beyond the possibility of serious question.

The Hague conventions stand by themselves. They have accomplished a certain amount—although only a small amount— of actual good. This was in so far as they furnished means by which nations which did not wish to quarrel were able to settle international disputes not involving their deepest interests. Questions between nations continually arise which are not of first-class importance; which, for instance, refer to some illegal act by or against a fishing schooner, to some difficulty concerning contracts, to some question of the interpretation of a minor clause in a treaty, or to the sporadic action of some hot-headed or panic-struck official.

In these cases, where neither nation wishes to go to war, the Hague Court has furnished an easy method for the settlement of the dispute without war. This does not mark a very great advance; but it is an advance, and was worth making.

THE CULT OF COWARDICE.

The fact that it is the only advance that the Hague Court has accomplished makes the hysterical outbursts formerly indulged in by the ultra-pacificists concerning it seem in retrospect exceedingly foolish. While I had never shared the hopes of these ultra-pacificists, I had hoped for more substantial good than has actually come from the Hague conventions. This was because I accept promises as meaning something.

The ultra-pacificists, whether from timidity, from weakness or from sheer folly, seem wholly unable to understand that the fulfilment of a promise has anything to do with making the promise.

The most striking example that could possibly be furnished has been furnished by Belgium. Under my direction as President, the United States signed the Hague conventions. All the nations engaged in the present war signed these conventions, although one or two of the nations qualified their acceptance, or withheld their signatures to certain articles.

This, however, did not in the least relieve the signatory powers from the duty to guarantee one another in the enjoyment of the rights supposed to be secured by the conventions.

To make this guarantee worth anything, it was, of course, necessary actively to enforce it against any power breaking the convention or acting against its clear purpose. To make it really effective it should be enforced as quickly against non-signatory as against signatory powers; for to give a power free permission to do wrong if it did not sign would put a premium on non-signing, so far as big, aggressive powers are concerned.

I authorised the signature of the United States to these conventions. They forbid the violation of neutral territory, and, of course, the subjugation of unoffending neutral nations, as Belgium has been subjugated.

They forbid such destruction as that inflicted on Louvain, Dinant, and other towns in Belgium, the burning of their priceless public libraries and wonderful halls and churches, and the destruction of cathedrals such as that at Rheims.

They forbid the infliction of heavy pecuniary penalties and the taking of severe punitive measures at the expense of civilian populations. They forbid the bombardment—of course the dropping of bombs from aeroplanes—of unfortified cities and of cities whose defences were not at the moment attacked.

All of these offences have been committed by Germany. I took the action I did in directing these conventions to be signed on the theory and with the belief that the United States intended to live up to its obligations, and that our people understood that living up to solemn obligations, like any other serious performance of duty, meant willingness to make effort and to incur risk.

If I had for one moment supposed that signing these Hague conventions meant literally nothing whatever beyond the expression of a pious wish which any power was at liberty to disregard with impunity, in accordance with the dictation of self-interest, I would certainly not have permitted the United States to be a party to such a mischievous farce.

President Wilson and Secretary Bryan, however, take the view that when the United States assumes obligations in order to secure small and unoffending neutral nations against hideous wrong, its action is not predicated on any intention to make the guarantee effective.

32

They take the view that when we are asked to redeem in the concrete promises we made in the abstract, our duty is to disregard our obligations and to preserve ignoble peace for ourselves by regarding with cold-blooded and timid indifference the most frightful ravages of war committed at the expense of a peaceful and unoffending country.

This is the cult of cowardice. That President Wilson and Mr. Bryan profess it and put it in action would be of small consequence if only they themselves were concerned. The importance of their action is that it commits the United States.

FORSAKING THE CAUSE OF PEACE.

Elaborate technical arguments have been made to justify this timid and selfish abandonment of duty, this timid and selfish failure to work for the world peace of righteousness, by President Wilson and Secretary Bryan. No sincere believer in disinterested and self-sacrificing work for peace can justify it; and work

33   c

for peace will never be worth much unless accompanied by courage, effort, and self-sacrifice.

Yet those very apostles of pacificism who, when they can do so with safety, scream loudest for peace, have made themselves objects of contemptuous derision by keeping silence in this crisis, or even by praising Mr. Wilson and Mr. Bryan for having thus abandoned the cause of peace.

They are supported by the men who insist that all that we are concerned with is ourselves escaping even the smallest risk that might follow upon the performance of duty to anyone except ourselves. This last is not a very exalted plea. It is, however, defensible. But if as a nation we intend to act in accordance with it, we must never promise to do anything for anyone else.

The technical arguments as to the Hague conventions not requiring us to act will at once be brushed aside by any man who honestly and in good faith faces the situation. Either the Hague conventions meant something or else they meant nothing. If in the event of their violation none of the signatory powers were even to protest, then of course they meant nothing; and it was an act of unspeakable silliness to enter into them.

If, on the other hand, they meant anything whatsoever, it was the duty of the United States, as the most powerful, or at least the richest and most populous neutral nation, to take action for upholding them when their violation brought such appalling disaster to Belgium. There is no escape from this alternative.

THE BAD FAITH OF THE UNITED STATES.

The first essential to working out successfully any scheme whatever for world peace is to understand that nothing can be accomplished unless the powers entering into the agreement act in precisely the reverse way from that in which President Wilson and Secretary Bryan have acted as regards the

Hague conventions and the all-inclusive arbitration treaties during the past six months.

The prime factor to consider in securing any peace agreement worth entering into, or that will have any except a mischievous effect, is that the nations entering into the agreement shall make no promises that ought not to be made, that they shall in good faith live up to the promises that are made, and that they shall put their whole strength unitedly back of these promises against any nation which refuses to carry out the agreement, or which, if it has not made the agreement, nevertheless violates the principles which the agreement enforces.

In other words, an international agreement that is to produce peace must proceed much along the lines of the Hague conventions; but a power signing them, as the United States signed them, must do so with the intention in good faith to see that they are carried out, and to use force to accomplish this, if necessary.

To violate these conventions, to violate neutrality treaties, as Germany has done in the case of Belgium, is a dreadful wrong. It represents the gravest kind of international wrongdoing, but it is really not quite so contemptible, it does not show such short-sighted and timid inefficiency, *and, above all, such selfish indifference to the cause of permanent and righteous peace*, as has been shown by the United States in refusing to fulfil its solemn obligations by taking whatever action was necessary in order to clear our skirts from the guilt of tame acquiescence in a wrong which we had solemnly undertaken to oppose.

It has been a matter of very real regret to me to have to speak in the way I have felt obliged to speak as to German wrongdoing in Belgium, because so many of my friends, not only Germans, but Americans of German birth and even Americans of German descent, have felt aggrieved at my position.

As regards my friends the Americans of German birth or descent, I can only say that they are in honour bound to regard all international matters solely from the standpoint of the interest of the United States, and of the demands of a lofty international morality.

As regards Germany, my stand is for the real interest of the mass of the German people. If the German people as a whole would only look at it rightly, they would see that my position is predicated upon the assumption that we ought to act as unhesitatingly in favour of Germany if Germany were wronged as we would act in favour of Belgium when Belgium was wronged.

There are in Germany a certain number of Germans who adopt the Trietschke and Bernhardi view of Germany's destiny and of international morality generally. These men are fundamentally exactly as hostile to America as to all other foreign powers, and I call the attention of my fellow Americans of German origin who wish this country to act toward Belgium, not in accordance with American traditions, interests, and ideals, but in accordance with the pro-German sympathies of certain citizens of German descent, to the statement of Trietschke that "to civilisation at large the [Americanising] of the German-Americans means a heavy loss. Among Germans there can no longer be any question that the civilisation of mankind suffers every time a German is transformed into a Yankee."

I do not for one moment believe that the men who follow Trietschke in his hatred of and contempt for all non - Germans, and Bernhardi in his contempt for international morality, are a majority of the German people or even a very large minority. I think that the great majority of the Germans, who have approved Germany's action towards Belgium, have been influenced by the feeling that it was a vital necessity in order to save Germany from destruction and subjugation by France and Russia, perhaps assisted by England.

Fear of national destruction will prompt men to do almost anything, and the proper remedy for outsiders to work for is the removal of the fear. If Germany were absolutely freed from danger of the least aggression on her eastern and western frontiers, I believe that German public sentiment would refuse to sanction such acts as those against Belgium.

The only effective way to free it from this fear is to have outside nations like the United States in good faith undertake the obligation to defend Germany's honour and territorial integrity if attacked, exactly as they would defend the honour and territorial integrity of Belgium, or of France, Russia, or England, or any other well-behaved, civilised power, if attacked.

PEACE WITHOUT RIGHTEOUSNESS.

This can only be achieved by some such world league of peace as that which I advocate. Most important of all, it can only be achieved by the willingness and ability of great, free powers to put might back of right, to make their protest against wrong-doing effective by, if necessary, punishing the wrongdoer.

WHY AMERICA SHOULD JOIN THE ALLIES.

It is this fact which makes the clamour of the pacificists for "Peace, Peace," without any regard to righteousness, so contemptible and so abhorrent to all right-thinking people. There are multitudes of professional pacificists in the United States, and of well-meaning but ill-informed persons who sympathise with them from ignorance.

There are not a few astute persons who wish to take sinister advantage of the folly of these persons, in the interest of Germany. All of these men clamour for immediate peace. They wish the United States to take action for immediate peace or for a truce, under conditions designed to leave Belgium with her wrongs unredressed and in the possession of Germany.

They strive to bring about a peace which would contain within itself the elements of frightful future disaster, by making no effective provision to prevent the repetition of such wrongdoing as has been inflicted upon Belgium. All of the men advocating such action, including the professional pacificists, the big business men largely of foreign birth, and the well-meaning but feeble-minded creatures among their allies—and including especially all those who from sheer timidity or weakness shrink from duty—occupy a thoroughly base and improper position.

The peace advocates of this stamp stand on an exact par with men who, if there were an epidemic of lawlessness in New York, should come together to demand the immediate cessation of all activity by the police, and should propose to substitute for it a request that the highwaymen and burglars cease their activities for the moment on condition of retaining undisturbed possession of the ill-gotten spoils they had already acquired.

The only effective friend of peace in a big city is the man who makes the police force thoroughly efficient, who tries to remove the causes of crime, but who unhesitatingly insists upon the punishment of criminals. Pacificists who believe that all use of force in inter-

national matters can be abolished will do well
to remember that the only efficient police
forces are those whose members are scrupu-
lously careful not to commit acts of violence
when it is possible to avoid them, but who are
willing and able, when the occasion arises, to
subdue the worst kind of wrongdoer by means
of the only argument that wrongdoer respects,
namely, successful force.   What is thus true
in private life is similarly true in international
affairs.

A WORKABLE PEACE PLAN.

No man can venture to state the exact
details that should be followed in securing
such a world league for the peace of righteousness.   But, not to leave the matter nebulous,
I submit the following plan.

It would prove entirely workable, if nations
entered into it with good faith, and if they
treated their obligations under it in the spirit
in which the United States treated its obligations as regarded the independence of Cuba,

giving good government to the Philippines,
and building the Panama Canal; the same
spirit in which England acted when the
neutrality of Belgium was violated.

All the civilised powers which are able and
willing to furnish and to use force, when force
is required to back up righteousness—and only
the civilised powers who possess virile manli-
ness of character and the willingness to accept
risk and labour, when necessary to the performance of duty, are entitled to be considered
in this matter—should join to create an international tribunal and to provide rules in
accordance with which that tribunal should
act.

These rules would have to accept the *status
quo* at some given period; for the endeavour to
redress all historical wrongs would throw us
back into chaos. They would lay down the
rule that the territorial integrity of each nation
was inviolate; that it was to be guaranteed
absolutely its sovereign rights in certain par-
ticulars, including, for instance, the right to

decide the terms on which immigrants should be admitted to its borders for purposes of residence, citizenship, or business; in short, all its rights in matters affecting its honour and vital interest. Each nation should be guaranteed against having any of these specified rights infringed upon.

They would not be made arbitrable, any more than an individual's right to life and limb is made arbitrable; they would be mutually guaranteed.

All other matters that could arise between these nations should be settled by the international court. The judges should act not as national representatives, but purely as judges, and in any given case it would probably be well to choose them by lot, excluding, of course, the representatives of the powers whose interests were concerned. Then, and most important, the nations should severally guarantee to use their entire military force, if necessary, against any nation which defied the decrees of the tribunal or which violated any of the rights which in the rules it was expressly stipulated should be reserved to the several nations, the rights to their territorial integrity and the like.

Under such conditions—to make matters concrete—Belgium would be safe from any attack such as that made by Germany, and Germany would be relieved from the haunting fear its people now have lest the Russians and the French, backed by other nations, smash the Empire and its people.

BENEFICIARIES OF THE PLAN.

In addition to the contracting powers, a certain number of outside nations should be named as entitled to the benefits of the court. These nations should be chosen from those which were as civilised and well-behaved as the great contracting nations, but which, for some reason or other, were unwilling or unable to guarantee to help execute the decrees of the court by force.

They would have no right to take part in

the nomination of judges, for no people are entitled to do anything towards establishing a court unless they are able and willing to face the risk, labour, and self-sacrifice necessary in order to put police power behind the court.

But they would be treated with exact justice, and in the event of any one of the great contracting powers having trouble with one of them, they would be entitled to go into court, have a decision rendered, and see the decision supported precisely as in the case of a dispute between any two of the great contracting powers themselves.

CIVILISATION A PREREQUISITE.

No power should be admitted into the first circle, that of the contracting powers, unless it was civilised, well-behaved, and able to do its part in enforcing the decrees of the court. China, for instance, could not be admitted, nor could Turkey, although for different reasons, whereas Germany, France, England, Italy, Russia, the United States, Japan, Brazil, the

Argentine, Chile, Uruguay, Switzerland, Holland, Sweden, Norway, Denmark, and Belgium would all be entitled to go in.

If China continues to behave as well as it has during the last few years it might perfectly well go into the second line of powers which were entitled to the benefits of the court, although not entitled to send judges to it. Mexico would, of course, not be entitled to admission at present into either circle.

At present, every European power with the exception of Turkey would be so entitled; but sixty years ago the kingdom of Naples, for instance, would not have been entitled to come in, and there are various South American communities which at the present time would not be entitled to come in; and, of course, this would at present be true of most independent Asiatic states and of all independent African states.

The council should have power to exclude any nation which completely fell from civilisation, as Mexico, partly with the able assistance of President Wilson's administration, has fallen during the past few years. There are various South and Central American states which have never been entitled to such consideration as civilised, orderly, self-respecting powers as would entitle them to be treated on terms of equality in the fashion indicated.

As regards these disorderly and weak outsiders, it might well be that after a while some method would be devised to deal with them by common agreement of the civilised powers; but until this was devised and put into execution they would have to be left as at present.

Of course, grave difficulties would be encountered in devising such a plan and in administering it afterwards, and no human being can guarantee that it would absolutely succeed. But I believe that it could be made to work and that it would mark a very great improvement over what obtains now. At this moment there is hell in Belgium and hell in Mexico; and the ultra - pacificists in this country have their full share of the responsibility for this hell. They are not primary factors in producing it. They lack the virile power to the primary factors in producing anything, good or evil, that needs daring and endurance. But they are secondary factors, for the man who tamely acquiesces in wrongdoing is a secondary factor in producing that wrongdoing. Most certainly the proposed plan would be dependent upon reasonable good faith for its successful working, but this is only to say what is also true of every human institution. Under the proposed plan there would be a strong likelihood of bettering world conditions. If it is a Utopia, it is a Utopia of a very practical kind.

FATUOUS INDIFFERENCE TO FACTS.

Such a plan is as yet in the realm of mere speculation. At present the essential thing for each self-respecting, liberty-loving nation to do is to put itself in position to defend its own rights. Recently President Wilson, in his message to Congress, has announced that we are in no danger and will not be in any danger; and ex-President Taft has stated that the awakening of interest in our defences indicates " mild hysteria."

Such utterances show fatuous indifference to the teachings of history. They represent precisely the attitude which a century ago led up to the burning of Washington by a small expeditionary hostile force, and to such paralysing disaster in war as almost to bring about the break-up of the Union.

In his message President Wilson justifies a refusal to build up our navy by asking—as if we were discussing a question of pure metaphysics—" When will the experts tell us just what kind of ships we should construct—and when will they be right for ten years together? Who shall tell us now what sort of navy to build? " and actually adds, after proposing and leaving unanswered these questions : " I turn away from the subject. It is not new. There is no need to discuss it."

If during its last ten years England's attitude towards preparedness for war and the upbuilding of her navy had been determined by statesmanship such as is set forth in these utterances of President Wilson, the island would now be trampled into bloody mire, as Belgium has been trampled.

If Germany had followed such advice—or rather no-advice—during the last ten years, she would now have been wholly unable so much as to assert her rights anywhere.

Let us immediately make our navy thoroughly efficient; and this can only be done by reversing the policy that President Wilson has followed for twenty-two months.

Neither our foreign affairs nor our naval affairs can be satisfactorily managed when our President is willing to put in their respective departments gentlemen like Mr. Bryan and Mr. Daniels. President Wilson would not have ventured to make either of these men head of the Treasury Department, because he would thereby have offended the concrete interests of American business men. But as Secretary of State and Secretary of the Navy the harm they do is to the country as a whole.

No concrete interest is immediately affected; and, as it is only our own common welfare in the future, only the welfare of our children, only the honour and interest of the United States through the generations that is concerned, it is deemed safe to disregard this welfare and to take chances with our national honour and interest.

THEODORE ROOSEVELT.

APPENDIX.

THE HAGUE CONVENTION

THE
HAGUE CONVENTION.

THE following extracts from the Final Act of
the Second Peace Conference, held at the Hague
in 1907, are given to enable the reader of Mr.
Roosevelt's article to understand more clearly
the reasons for his arguments.   It will be
observed that Germany during the present
war has violated many of the main articles of
the Convention to which she was a party,
bearing on war on land, on sea, and in the
air.

In his article Mr. Roosevelt says : " While
I had never shared the hopes of ultra-pacificists,
I had hoped for more substantial good than has
actually come from the Hague Convention.
This was because I accept promises as mean-
ing something.   Under my directions as Presi-
dent, the United States signed the Hague
Convention."

The irony of the first part of these words

is best emphasised by comparing what Germany has done in this war with what she promised to abstain from doing at the Hague Conference.

AMERICA CONVENED THE PEACE CONFERENCE.

The following extract from the British Blue Book containing the full report of the Conference contains, in view of America's present attitude as set forth by Mr. Roosevelt, one outstanding fact—the fact that the United States Government were the leaders in bringing about the Conference:

THE Second International Peace Conference, proposed in the first instance by the President of the United States of America, having been convoked, on the invitation of His Majesty the Emperor of All the Russias, by Her Majesty the Queen of the Netherlands, assembled on the 15th of June, 1907, at The Hague, in the Hall of the Knights, for the purpose of giving a fresh development to the humanitarian principles which served as a basis for the work of the First Conference of 1899.

In addition to the United States, the following powers, among others, signed the

Hague Convention : Germany, Austria-Hungary, Belgium, France, Great Britain, Italy, Japan, Luxemburg, Montenegro, Persia, Portugal, Roumania, Russia, Servia, and Turkey. A few of the articles of the Convention were not agreed to by certain of the signatory powers, however.

NEUTRAL TERRITORY.

The Convention forbids the violation of neutral territory, as laid down in the following articles on the Rights and Duties of Neutral Powers :

ARTICLE 1.
The territory of neutral Powers inviolable.

ARTICLE 2.
Belligerents are forbidden to move troops or convoys, whether of munitions of war or of supplies, across the territory of a neutral Power.

ARTICLE 10.
The fact of a neutral Power resisting, even by force, attempts to violate its neutrality cannot be regarded as a hostile act.

It also forbids wanton and unnecessary destruction and pillage:

ARTICLE 27.

In sieges and bombardments all necessary steps must be taken to spare, as far as possible, buildings dedicated to public worship, art, science, or charitable purposes, historic monuments, hospitals, and places where the sick and wounded are collected, provided they are not being used at the time for military purposes.

It is the duty of the besieged to indicate such buildings or places by distinctive and visible signs, which shall be notified to the enemy beforehand.

ARTICLE 28.

The giving over to pillage of a town or place, even when taken by assault, is forbidden.

Germany agreed to these conditions—before the war. How she has kept her promises is now obvious to the whole world.

The infliction of heavy money penalties and the taking of severe punitive measures at the expense of civilian populations is expressly forbidden:

ARTICLE 50.

No collective penalty, pecuniary or otherwise, shall be inflicted upon the population on account of the acts of individuals for which it cannot be regarded as collectively responsible.

BOMBARDING UNDEFENDED PLACES.

By the terms of the Hague Convention the bombardment, including the dropping of bombs from aircraft, of unfortified cities and places, is not permissible:

ARTICLE 25.

The attack or bombardment, by any means whatever, of undefended towns, villages, dwellings, or buildings, is forbidden.

The Contracting Powers agree to prohibit, for a period extending to the close of the Third Peace Conference, the discharge of projectiles and explosives from balloons or by other new methods of a similar nature.

The bombardment by naval forces of undefended ports, towns, villages, dwellings, or buildings is forbidden.

Mr. Roosevelt does not make mention of every way in which the Germans have violated the Hague Conventions. For instance, it is particularly forbidden:

(*f.*) To make improper use of a flag of truce, of the national flag, or of the military insignia and uniform of the enemy, as well as of the distinctive signs of the Geneva Convention;

(*g.*) To destroy or seize enemy property, unless such destruction or seizure be imperatively demanded by the necessities of war.

It is also decreed by the Convention that:

Family honour and rights, individual life, and private property, as well as religious convictions and worship, must be respected.

Private property may not be confiscated.

DESTROYING ART TREASURES.

In view of the destruction of Louvain and Dinant and other towns, and the shelling of Rheims Cathedral by the Germans, the following extracts from the Convention may be quoted with particular force :

The property of local authorities, as well as that of institutions dedicated to public worship, charity, education, and to science and art, and even when State property, shall be treated as private property.

Any seizure or destruction of, or wilful damage to, institutions of this character, historic monuments and works of science and art, is forbidden, and should be made the subject of legal proceedings.

MINES IN THE SEA.

With regard to the mining of the North Sea and other sea areas by the Germans, whose representatives at the Conference alone stood out against the prohibition of mines, the following regulations for the employment of automatic contact submarine mines were agreed upon :

ARTICLE 1.

It is forbidden:

1. To lay unanchored automatic contact mines, unless they be so constructed as to become harmless one hour at most after the person who laid them has ceased to control them;

2. To lay anchored automatic contact mines which do not become harmless as soon as they have broken loose from their moorings;

ARTICLE 3.

When anchored automatic contact mines are employed, every possible precaution must be taken for the security of peaceful shipping.

The belligerents undertake to do their utmost to render these mines harmless after a limited time has elapsed, and, should the mines cease to be under observation, to notify the danger zones as soon as military exigencies permit by a notice to mariners, which must also be communicated to the Governments through the diplomatic channel.

NEUTRAL TRADING.

The question of supplies from a neutral power to a belligerent power, a question at present under discussion between Great Britain and the United States, is dealt with as follows:

ARTICLE 6.

The supply, in any manner, directly or indirectly, of war-ships, supplies, or war material of any kind whatever, by a neutral Power to a belligerent Power, is forbidden.

ARTICLE 7.

A neutral Power is not bound to prevent the export or transit, for either belligerent, of arms, munitions of war, or, in general, of anything which could be of use to an army or fleet.

ARTICLE 25.

A neutral Power is bound to exercise such vigilance as the means at its disposal permit to prevent any violation of the provisions of the above Articles occurring in its ports or roadsteads or in its waters.

It will be seen from the above extracts, read in conjunction with Mr. Roosevelt's article, that he is justified in urging something more than mere passive neutrality on the part of the United States.

370055

Made in the USA